ENGLISH ELECTRIC

Martin Hart

AMBERLEY

First published 2014

Amberley Publishing
The Hill, Stroud
Gloucestershire, GL5 4EP

www.amberley-books.com

Copyright © Martin Hart, 2014

The right of Martin Hart to be identified as the Author of this work has been
asserted in accordance with the Copyrights, Designs and Patents Act 1988.

ISBN 978 1 4456 3340 4 (print)
ISBN 978 1 4456 3351 0 (ebook)

British Library Cataloguing in Publication Data.
A catalogue record for this book is available from the British Library.

Typeset in 11pt on 12pt Sabon LT Std.
Typesetting by Amberley Publishing.
Printed in the UK.

ABOUT THE AUTHOR

My interest in diesel locomotives of British Railways started back in the late 1970s. Due to the costly nature of photography for someone who was young back then, it was only in 1984, when I had finally saved up enough money to purchase my first SLR camera, that I started making a

The author alongside 50031 *Hood* during a driver experience course at the Severn Valley Railway in 2013.

photographic record of what I saw. This coincided, however, with the time that my interest began to wane and it was not until 20 years later that my interest was rekindled when I stumbled across some of my old pictures of locomotives from the 1980s while looking for something in our loft.

I scanned some of these photographs, primarily to ensure that I had electronic copies before they degraded any further. My interest rekindled, I did a bit of research on the Internet and found that in the intervening years there had been many changes – many of my favourite classes of locomotive (invariably a product of English Electric) had been scrapped. On the positive side, however, there existed a thriving diesel preservation movement, with many preserved locomotives operating on the host of privately owned heritage railways across the country. There were also many very active Internet forums and websites. Within these, people discussed the state of current projects, recounted tales of the past, and shared photographs of currently preserved locomotives as well as those taken years ago.

Since 2004 I have begun to follow the surviving members of some classic English Electric diesel locomotive designs from my youth. Having bought a better-quality camera, I am now in a position to record their existence, both in preservation and during their restoration following their withdrawal from British Rail (BR). It is this that is the main focus of this book.

I am a member of The Fifty Fund and have shares in a number of preserved Class 50 locomotives.

THE ENGLISH ELECTRIC COMPANY

The English Electric Company had a long pedigree as a great British industrial manufacturer. Initially specialising in the production of transformers and industrial electric motors, it gradually diversified and expanded to include the production of locomotive and traction equipment, steam turbines, computers, guided missiles and even jet aircraft.

English Electric was founded at the end of the First World War. In 1917 Dick, Kerr & Co., a partnership between the Glaswegian merchants W. B. Dick and John Kerr, acquired the United Electric Car Company, a tram manufacturer based in Preston, Lancashire. In 1918, The English Electric Company Limited was formed when this company took over diesel engine manufacturers Willans & Robinson of Rugby, the Phoenix Dynamo Manufacturing Company of Bradford, and the Stafford works of Siemens Brothers Dynamo Works Ltd.

The diverse nature of its constituent parts was such that the company could manufacture a wide variety of products. Initially, it concentrated its efforts on the manufacturing of industrial electric motors and transformers. By 1930, the manufacture of electrical equipment had been moved to Bradford, while the bus body, tram and rolling stock production remained in Preston.

From its earliest beginnings the company had been involved in the production of trams. By 1923 they began to diversify, and delivered electric locomotives to the New Zealand Railways for use in the Southern Alps. Between 1924 and 1926, English Electric also supplied nine electric locomotives to the Harbour Commissioners of Montreal, Canada. A year later, English Electric delivered an order for twenty electric motor cars for Warsaw's suburban light railway. During the 1930s, English Electric supplied equipment for the electrification of the Southern Railway (SR), thereby reinforcing its position in the home traction market.

In 1955 English Electric took over the Vulcan Foundry in Preston and the Darlington-based Robert Stephenson & Hawthorns, both of whom boasted enviable railway engineering pedigrees. It was from these two facilities, until the end of the 1960s, that English Electric produced almost 1,000 diesel and electric locomotives of nine different classes for British Railways. These were a result of the flurry of orders received in relation to the British Transport Commission's Modernisation Plan. Many of these classes provided decades of service, and some are still in active service in 2014 with current Train Operating Companies (TOCs).

LOCOMOTIVE PRODUCTION AND THE BRITISH TRANSPORT COMMISSION MODERNISATION PLAN

Historically the 'big four' railway companies – the London & North-Eastern Railway (LNER), Great Western Railway (GWR), Southern Railway (SR) and the London Midland & Scottish Railway (LMS) – had looked to develop more modern forms of traction than steam. However, it was only the LMS that had actually operated a main-line diesel locomotive in regular service before nationalisation in 1948. While experimentation continued on a sporadic and uncoordinated basis, a more national approach was adopted with the publication of the 1955 British Transport Commission's (BTC) fifteen-year modernisation plan for British Railways (BR). A significant element of the plan was to replace steam traction across the entire national railway network. As a precursor to this there was a requirement for 171 'Pilot Scheme' locomotives of thirteen differing types. It was envisaged that in-service trials of these could be undertaken to finalise the design and specifications of the new motive power, before the placing of orders as part of the plan.

British Railways, however, was still preoccupied with the construction and maintenance of its existing fleet of steam locomotives. This being

the case, it was left to private locomotive builders, some of whom had experience of diesel locomotive production for Commonwealth countries, to fill the need.

Diesel locomotives differ from steam in that they are seldom built as one unit, instead comprising a power unit, various electrical machines, running gear and bodywork. These components were often sourced from a variety of specialist manufacturers. One exception was English Electric, who not only designed and built their own power units, generators and traction units but also constructed complete locomotives.

Between 1955 and 1969 English Electric produced three iconic variants of diesel locomotive, classified using the British Railways system of horsepower as either Type 4 (2,000–2,999 hp) or Type 5 (3,000+ hp). Under the BR Total Operations Processing System (TOPS) of classification, these became known as Class 40, Class 50 and Class 55 'Deltic' locomotives.

ENGLISH ELECTRIC TYPE 4 (BRITISH RAIL CLASS 40): 1958–85

The origins of the Class 40 locomotives can be traced back to some of the earliest main-line diesel locomotive designs. British Railways Class D16/1 (10000 and 10001) had been the first mainline diesel locomotive type in the UK. These locomotives had been designed and built at Derby Locomotive Works between 1947 and 1948 by the English Electric Company, using parts designed by Henry George Ivatt – the post-war Chief Mechanical Engineer of the LMS. The locomotives made use of the English Electric EE16SVT Mk I 1,600-hp diesel engine coupled to a DC generator for electric transmission. The engine itself was a pressure-charged version of a very successful, naturally aspirated English Electric design that had previously been used in its standard diesel-electric shunting locomotives.

Similarly, BR Class D16/2 was a class of prototype diesel locomotive built at its Ashford Works and introduced slightly later, in 1950–1, with a third example in 1954. Oliver Bulleid had designed all three for the Southern Railway (SR) before nationalisation in 1948. Like the LMS designs, 10201 and 10202 made use of the English Electric EE16SVT Mk I diesel engine and transmission. Number 10203, built by British Railways at its Brighton works, emerged a few years later, and had a modified EE16SVT Mk II power unit, giving a power output of 2,000 hp. It was this, together with the bogie design, that was used in an unchanged form on the first ten production Class 40 locomotives.

BR ordered ten English Electric Type 4s (later known as Class 40s) as evaluation prototypes. Constructed at the Vulcan Foundry in Newton-le-Willows, Lancashire, the first locomotive (D200) was delivered to Stratford in March 1958. D200 made its first public appearance on a demonstration run from London Liverpool Street to Norwich on 18 April 1958.

Although the first ten prototypes had met with varying degrees of success, BR felt that they had proved their worth, and so ordered a further 190 examples (D210–D399). The majority were constructed at the Vulcan Foundry, with the exception of a small batch of twenty (D305–D324). These were built at the Robert Stephenson & Hawthorns factory in Darlington, while Vulcan Foundry concentrated on the short production run of the Class 55 'Deltics'. All locomotives were painted in all-over Brunswick green livery; the final one was delivered in September 1962. Initially, class members lacked a high-visibility warning on their front ends – although a rectangular yellow warning panel was applied at a later date.

During their four years of construction, different batches of the class showed significant design differences due to changes in BR working practices.

The first 125 locomotives (D200–D324) were built with central gangway doors, to allow train crew to move between locomotives in multiple, and headcode disc markers, by which BR identified services. Later, it was decided that locomotives should display the four-character train reporting headcode of the service they were hauling. In order to accommodate this change, examples numbered D325–D344 were built with split headcode boxes, one either side of the locomotive's central gangway doors. A further policy decision led to the abandonment of gangway doors on locomotives, and so the final examples D345–D399 were constructed with a single, centrally positioned four-character headcode box. This gave the locomotive a much cleaner and uncluttered look to its cab ends.

Although the class was large in number, very few were given names. Between April 1960 and March 1963, twenty-five of the London Midland Region fleet, numbers D210–D225 and D226–D235, were given names, all of which related to ocean liners belonging to Cunard, Elder Dempster Lines and Canadian Pacific, and all associated with the port of Liverpool. The first three locomotives D210–D212 had official naming ceremonies, while the others received their nameplates during works visits. The nameplates themselves were possibly the most stylish to ever adorn a BR diesel locomotive, having both the name and an integral roundel containing the flag of the ocean liner company. Locomotive D226 was officially allocated the name *Media*, but for some reason it was never applied. During the early 1970s the nameplates began to vanish from the locomotives – their removal not always being for legitimate reasons.

In the early 1980s, some of the previously named class members had their original names stencilled on to their bodysides by nostalgic depot staff. Some versions were neatly applied in the same position that the original nameplates had once been located, using white paint on a red background – thereby having a passing resemblance to a proper nameplate.

With the introduction of the BR Total Operations Processing System (TOPS) in 1973, the locomotives were designated Class 40 and renumbered accordingly 40001–40199. Locomotives D201–D399 were renumbered in sequence. Pioneer D200, the first-built locomotive, was renumbered 40122, as this number was vacant due to the scrapping of D322 after a serious accident at Acton Grange Junction on 13 May 1966.

The early 1960s saw the heyday of the class, when they hauled express passenger services on the West Coast Main Line (WCML) and in East Anglia. Once teething troubles had been eradicated, locomotive crews and fitters alike had a particular fondness for the class. However, the arrival of more powerful classes of locomotive, such as the English Electric Class 55 'Deltics', together with the electrification of the WCML, meant that the fleet was soon relegated to more mundane passenger services and freight duties. While the last of the class were entering service, they had already been replaced on top-link duties – being considered underpowered and overweight compared to more contemporary designs.

Arguably the most notorious class member was D326 (40126). On 26 December 1962, while hauling the 'Midday Scot' from Glasgow to Euston, it ran in to the rear of another passenger train. Eighteen passengers were killed and thirty-three seriously injured. On the night of 8 August 1963, while working the Aberdeen/Glasgow–Euston Royal Mail train, the same locomotive was involved in the infamous 'Great Train Robbery', where thieves flagged the train down and made off with approximately £2.6 million. A year later, in August 1964, D326 was again implicated in a fatality, when a young secondman, having gained access by opening the doors on top of the nose to clean the front windscreens, came into contact with overhead wires and was electrocuted. Finally, in August 1965, while approaching Birmingham New Street, the locomotive suffered a total brake failure. Signalling staff swiftly diverted the locomotive into another platform where it ran in to the back of a goods train, injuring the guard but avoiding a major accident. When 40126 was finally withdrawn by BR in February 1984, it was decided to offer it no chance for a reprieve (or an opportunity for souvenir-hunters), and it was cut up almost immediately at Doncaster Works in April 1984.

With the introduction of carriages equipped with electric train heating (ETH), passenger workings by the class started to diminish as a result of their lack of this capability. The class tended to operate on secondary passenger duties, summer holiday trains, parcel traffic and heavy freight trains. Members of the class could be found working over a large geographical area, ranging from the Midlands up to the north of Scotland, North Wales and as far south as Severn Tunnel Junction. The only regions not familiar with Class 40s were the Southern Region and the more westerly parts of the Western Region.

In 1980 they lost their last front-line passenger duties in Scotland. Their last regular use on passenger workings was on the North Wales Coast Line between Holyhead, Crewe and Manchester. Throughout the early 1980s, Class 40s were still regularly seen on day excursion and holidaymaker services – their lack of electric train heating being far less of an issue.

Withdrawals began as early as 1976 when three members of the class were taken out of service. Many had not been converted to dual braking, and the lack of air brakes on some examples made them incapable of being used on more modern freight and passenger vehicles. Despite this, only seventeen of the class had been withdrawn by the start of the 1980s. From then onwards, the rate of withdrawals began to increase, as they were a valuable source of spare parts, with non-air-braked examples being the first to be earmarked. By 1981, the remaining 130 locomotives were concentrated in the London Midland Region of BR. Classified works overhauls on Class 40s were phased out, with only twenty-nine members of the class receiving attention in 1980, the final two appearing from Crewe works in 1981.

Class numbers shrank year-on-year, until by 1984 only sixteen examples remained operational. Included in this number was the original D200 (now 40122), which, although having been withdrawn in 1981, was spotted by two keen followers on the scrap line at Carlisle Kingmoor (KD) depot in readiness for its scrapping at Swindon Works. Thanks to their efforts and persuasiveness, 40122 was reinstated by BR and overhauled at Toton (TO) depot with parts from 40076. It was reinstated in July 1983 and painted in its original BR Brunswick green livery again, primarily to haul enthusiasts' rail tours and special charter work, although it was also used on normal passenger workings.

The last Class 40 passenger working was on 27 January 1985, when 40012 hauled the Birmingham New Street–York service. All remaining locomotives, with the exception of 40122, were withdrawn the next day. However, in a somewhat bizarre turn of events, four locomotives (40012, 40060, 40118 and 40135) were temporarily reinstated and found use on engineering trains for the remodelling project of Crewe station. These locomotives were given a Class 97 departmental numbering in the range 97405–97408. Upon completion of the project, the four locomotives continued in active service, working a variety of ballast and freight trains until finally being withdrawn by March 1987. Three of the four departmental locos were offered to preservation groups. Sadly, 40060 did not survive, and was scrapped at Vic Berry's in Leicester during March 1988. In the same year, 40122 was finally withdrawn and presented to the National Railway Museum (NRM), where it currently resides, for preservation.

Many of the Class 40 fleet met their demise either at Crewe, Doncaster or Swindon Works. The very last examples to be cut up were 40091 and 40195 at Crewe works in December 1988. Currently, just seven examples from the original total of 200 survive in various states of repair from operational and certified for use on the national main line to those requiring many years of restoration work.

On 30 November 2002, class member 40145, now owned by the Class 40 Preservation Society, hauled an enthusiasts' rail tour from Crewe to Holyhead and back. This was the first time a Class 40 had hauled a main-line passenger train for over sixteen years.

40012 *Aureol* (as D212) at Swanwick Junction on the Midland Railway–Butterley during a running day in 2008.

40012 *Aureol* stabled at Swanwick Junction on the Midland Railway–Butterley in 2009. Note the ladder attached to the nose, a feature on the first few examples of the class.

40012 *Aureol* stabled at Swanwick Junction on the Midland Railway–Butterley in 2011.

40013 *Andania* (as D213) on display at the Barrow Hill Roundhouse near Chesterfield in 2010.

40013 *Andania* on display at the Barrow Hill Roundhouse near Chesterfield in 2010. Note the full-yellow ends, as opposed to the yellow rectangle that was applied to some members of the class.

40106 (as D306) stands in the head-shunt at Wansford on the Nene Valley Railway during a diesel gala in 2009.

40106 runs round at Kidderminster Town on the Severn Valley Railway during a diesel gala in 2011. 40106 had recently undergone bodywork repairs, resulting in its complete repaint back to an as-new condition in Brunswick green with no front-end yellow warning panels.

40106 in profile, showing the nose and cab detail.

40106 awaits its next turn of duty at Ruddington Fields on the Great Central Railway (Nottingham) during a diesel gala in 2012.

40106 slows for Rushcliffe Halt on the Great Central Railway (Nottingham) during a diesel gala in 2012.

40118 undergoing a long-term restoration project at Birmingham Railway Museum, Tyseley, in 2005. It was one of twenty Class 40s built at the Robert Stephenson & Hawthorn factory in Darlington, allowing production capacity at the Vulcan Foundry to build the twenty-two production Class 55 Deltics.

40118 undergoing a long-term restoration project at Birmingham Railway Museum, Tyseley, in 2011. It shows little progress from the previous illustration, although an enormous amount of internal work has been undertaken in the intervening years.

40122 (as D200) under repair at the National Railway Museum (NRM) in 2008. D200 was famous for having been the first of the small batch of locomotives ordered under the pilot scheme for the British Transport Commission (BTC) 1955 Modernisation Plan.

40122 was exhibited (albeit in a less than pristine condition) at the National Railway Museum (NRM) during the 2012 Railfest celebrations.

40135 (as D335) stops at Ramsbottom on the East Lancashire Railway during a running day in 2011.

40135 on the buffer stops at Rawtenstall on the East Lancashire Railway in 2011. 40135 is the only preserved example of a split-headcode Class 40.

A comparison of English Electric Class 40 and Class 37 noses. 40135 and 37901 *Mirrlees Pioneer* at Bury Bolton Street on the East Lancashire Railway during a running day in 2012.

40135 at Bury Bolton Street on the East Lancashire Railway in 2013. The locomotive has a fully operational steam heating boiler, which can be seen to be in use.

40135 at Bury Bolton Street on the East Lancashire Railway during an English Electric-themed running day in 2014.

40145 (as 345) at Rawtenstall on the East Lancashire Railway in 2013. 40145 was one of the final Class 40s to receive a general overhaul at Crewe Works in November 1980. In February 1984 the locomotive was purchased by the Class 40 Preservation Society (CFPS) and became the first Class 40 to enter preservation.

40145 at Rawtenstall on the East Lancashire Railway in 2014. The locomotive is the only mainline-certified Class 40.

40145 at Rawtenstall on the East Lancashire Railway in 2014. It was the first locomotive of the final delivery batch from English Electric, which were constructed with a centrally positioned four-character headcode box.

ENGLISH ELECTRIC TYPE 4 CO-CO (BRITISH RAIL CLASS 50): 1967–1994

In 1965 British Rail (BR) had a need for some high-powered diesel locomotives. They were required in order to speed up services on the non-electrified portions of the West Coast Main Line (WCML) between Crewe and Glasgow, prior to completion of the electrification work. The relatively new Brush Sulzer Type 4 locomotives (later designated

50049 *Defiance* at Fishguard Harbour. Both this locomotive and 50031 *Hood* were leased to Arriva Trains Wales in order to provide motive power for regular service trains from Cardiff to Fishguard during the summer of 2006.

Class 47) were the obvious choice for this role, but were proving unreliable at the time due to engine problems.

At around the same time, English Electric had been experiencing success with a private venture in the form of DP2 (Diesel Prototype 2), a test bed for its new charge-cooled EE16CSVT engine. First delivered in May 1962, DP2 found itself on the East Coast Main Line (ECML), running alongside the production-line Deltic locomotives, where it was popular with crews (possibly due to the quietness in the cab compared to the production Deltics) and proved a capable performer. Visually, DP2 looked similar to the production Deltics, as it used the last bodyshell – that now being spare, the order having been reduced by one after it had been manufactured. As a result of its success, an order for a fleet of fifty locomotives was placed with English Electric, based on the DP2 power unit and mechanicals, but with a BR-designed bodyshell and additional electronic systems. The company were displeased that their proven electrical systems were to be compromised by the addition of unproven systems that had never before been tested in a locomotive environment. Such systems included dynamic braking, wheelslip protection, electronic power control with automatic control of tractive effort and slow speed control.

A squadron of fifty English Electric Type 4 Co-Co locomotives, initially numbered in the range D400–D449, were built at the English Electric Vulcan Foundry in Newton-le-Willows between 1967 and

1968. Initially, BR leased the fleet from English Electric to avoid capital costs, and it was not until 1973 that BR finally purchased the locomotives from the company. Initially there were problems with the EE16CSVT power units, resulting in poor availability. Newly designed cylinder heads were soon fitted to the fleet. Between 1969 and 1970, track improvements on the WCML allowed higher line speeds, so the locomotives began to work in multiple. Although all were wired for multiple working, only the first two examples (D400 and D401) had been fitted with their external front-mounted jumper cables from new. The remainder of the class had them fitted on a retrospective basis.

By 1974, the entire WMCL had been electrified, so the locomotives were redeployed as had been originally planned. The London Midland Region retained fifteen members of the class for passenger duties in

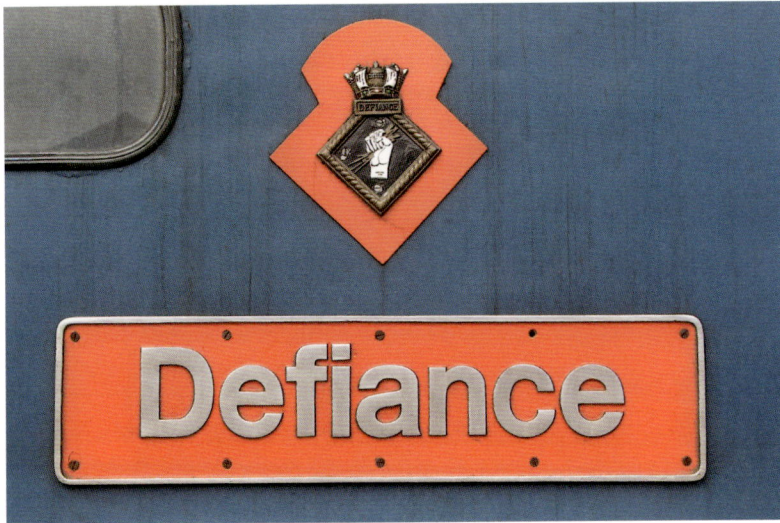

Nameplate and crest of 50049 *Defiance*.

North Wales and the North West. The remainder were allocated to Bristol Bath Road (BR), Laira (LA) and Old Oak Common (OC) depots in the Western Region as part of the drive to replace their diesel-hydraulic locomotives, which were seen as non-standard.

With the introduction of the BR Total Operations Processing System (TOPS) in 1973, the locomotives were designated Class 50 and renumbered accordingly in sequence 50001–50050, with D400 becoming 50050 due to a limitation of the system. An interesting development was seen in 1978 with the application of British warship names to the fleet. The names chosen were those of warships that had been part of the First World War or Second World War battle fleets, excluding those that had any association with the empire or royalty. The application of names to all the fleet met with general approval, and went a long way to diminish the previous anonymity of the class.

By the mid-1970s the class had again been hit with reliability issues, primarily due to the poor design of the internal air-management systems. The inertial air filters had been positioned too close to the exhaust ports, thereby collecting their fumes. In addition, there were problems with the unproven BR electronic systems, as foreseen by English Electric themselves during the design phase. This being the case, a refurbishment programme for the whole class, starting with 50006 *Neptune*, was undertaken at the Doncaster Works between 1979 and 1983.

During refurbishment, the headcode boxes and sandbox fillers were plated over, the bodyside window closest to the Number 1 end was replaced by a grille, and a high-intensity headlight was fitted to each cab end. The bulk of the work, however, concentrated on improving the engine room airflow, which included modifications to the roof and complex electronic equipment. It also resulted in the change of the inertial air filter by the main generator, which had produced the characteristic Class 50 sound – this earning the class the nickname of 'Hoovers' or 'vacs'. The most visible difference, however, was that of the new BR 'large logo' style of livery. This was applied to the seventh locomotive refurbished and to all those that followed. This new, bold livery with its wrap-around yellow ends, grey roof, full-height BR logo and large TOPS numerals really suited the shape of the locomotives and transformed their appearance.

In general, the refurbishment programme cured many of the common Class 50 issues and they began to provide a reliable service. The introduction of High Speed Trains (HSTs) on the Western Region in the late 1970s saw the Class 50s again relegated to secondary duties, and the class became associated with the Southern Region, where they replaced the native Class 33s. Network SouthEast inherited the majority of the fleet when BR underwent sectorisation in 1986. The remainder went to the Departmental Sector. Their transfer to Network SouthEast was accompanied by another change in their livery – an unpopular lighter blue body with white, red and grey body stripes. The class continued on the Waterloo–West of England, Paddington–Thames and Chiltern workings until being replaced in the early 1990s. These latter days were again plagued by reliability issues due to a combination of poor maintenance and the punishing nature of running at full power on a stop-start service pattern over worn track.

The year 1987 saw overhaul duties for the class transferred from Doncaster Works to Crewe Works. This relocation raised issues of a changed workforce having to learn the foibles of the class. Withdrawals started the same year, the first being 50011 *Centurion*. This example was sent to Crewe with the intention of it becoming a static engine test bed for overhauled power units. The locomotive had had less than four years' active service since its refurbishment at Doncaster Works. Crewe Works overhauled separate components of the locomotives and subsequently had them dispatched to Laira (LA) depot for fitting. Problems were often experienced when attempting to reattach delivered parts to locomotives. This further increased maintenance costs and worsened their availability rate. At a time when costs were being minimised, it was the end for the class under BR InterCity sector auspices. By 1989 this sector had removed all passenger-hauled diagrams for Class 50s. From here onwards, members of the class were withdrawn from service as they failed or became too expensive to repair, their parts robbed to keep others running. The final use of Class 50s in regular BR service was on 24 May 1992 with 50007 *Sir Edward Elgar* (previously *Hercules*) and 50050 *Fearless*. This pair, plus 50033 *Glorious*, was retained until early 1994 for use on enthusiasts' specials, such was the huge popularity of the class, not seen for over a decade since the demise of the Deltics.

Numbers 50007 and 50050 worked their final rail tour, 'The 50 Terminator', on 26 March 1994 with a run from London Waterloo to Penzance and back in to London Paddington. The locomotives were both withdrawn at the end of the month on the last day of BR existence, thereby becoming the final two members of the class to be withdrawn, after over twenty-six years of active service.

Many of the Class 50 fleet met their end at scrapyards; a few that were unable to be moved were simply cut up on site at their depot. Some, however, thanks to dedicated enthusiasts, have been preserved or are currently being restored for future generations at private railways across the country. Currently, eighteen examples from the original total of fifty survive in various states of repair from operational and certified for use on the national main line to others requiring many years of restoration work.

On 1 November 1997, 50031 *Hood*, now owned by The Fifty Fund, hauled 'The Pilgrim Hoover' rail tour. Staring from Birmingham International, it hauled a tour along its old stamping grounds – down to Plymouth, along the sea wall at Dawlish and over the South Devon Banks. The locomotive performed faultlessly throughout. This was the first time a Class 50 had hauled a main-line passenger train since their retirement from BR.

50002 *Superb* (as D402) undergoing long-term repairs and restoration at Buckfastleigh on the South Devon Railway in 2009.

50002 *Superb* cab end detail. The centrally located high-intensity headlight fitted to the cab end has been removed to give a pre-refurbishment appearance to the locomotive.

50007 *Sir Edward Elgar* stabled at Swanwick Junction on the Midland Railway–Butterley in 2009.

50007 *Sir Edward Elgar* at Leicester North on the Great Central Railway during a diesel gala in 2009.

50007 *Sir Edward Elgar* stops at Quorn & Woodhouse on the Great Central Railway during a diesel gala in 2010. In 2013 the locomotive was bought by the owner of locomotive 40106.

50008 *Thunderer* at Wansford on the Nene Valley Railway during a diesel gala in 2009. This was the first passenger duty for 50008 for over a decade, since an unsuccessful attempt to export it to Peru by its then owners.

50008 *Thunderer* stands at Bury Bolton Street on the East Lancashire Railway in 2010. This was the first outing for 50008 since it was repainted back into the BR Laira Blue livery it carried during its final years of service with BR.

50008 *Thunderer* stands outside its current home at Washwood Heath, Birmingham, in 2011.

Cab detail of 50008 *Thunderer*, showing the external front-mounted jumper cables for multiple working, and the centrally mounted high-intensity spotlight.

50008 *Thunderer* on shed at Wansford on the Nene Valley Railway during a diesel gala in 2013.

50015 *Valiant* at Bury Bolton Street on the East Lancashire Railway in 2008. This was one of its first outings, having been stored unserviceable for several years.

50015 *Valiant* at Haworth on the Keighley & Worth Valley Railway during a diesel gala in 2010. This was the first outing for 50015 for some time, the locomotive having undergone a series of repairs, together with a complete repaint in BR Large Logo livery.

50015 *Valiant* and 37901 *Mirrlees Pioneer* reach the end of the line at Oxenhope on the Keighley & Worth Valley Railway during a diesel gala in 2010.

50015 *Valiant* and 50044 *Exeter* run round the coaching stock at Rawtenstall on the East Lancashire Railway during a diesel gala in 2010.

50015 *Valiant* stabled at Ruddington Fields on the Great Central Railway (Nottingham) during a diesel gala in 2013. This was only the second time a member of the class had been a guest locomotive at this particular preserved railway – the first being 50007 *Sir Edward Elgar* back in 2003.

50017 *Royal Oak* awaits attention at Birmingham Railway Museum in 2004.

50017 *Royal Oak* stored at Birmingham Railway Museum in 2005. It is pictured here prior to its latest restoration, minus its nameplates and in maroon livery, a legacy from when it was hired to work the Venice Simplon Orient Express (VSOE) dining-car train services.

50017 *Royal Oak* undergoing repairs at Birmingham Railway Museum during 2007. Since this picture was taken, it has moved to the Plym Valley Railway and been restored to operational condition at a very high standard.

Cab detail of 50019 *Ramillies* together with a Hoover headboard.

50019 *Ramillies* at Dereham on the Mid-Norfolk Railway during a diesel gala in 2009.

50019 *Ramillies* at Dereham on the Mid-Norfolk Railway during a diesel gala in 2013. This was one of its final runs before a scheduled programme of heavy maintenance on the locomotive, which will involve it being out of service for a lengthy period.

50019 *Ramillies* in the head-shunt at Wymondham Abbey on the Mid-Norfolk Railway in 2013.

50021 *Rodney* stored unserviceable alongside 50017 *Royal Oak* at Birmingham Railway Museum in 2005.

50021 *Rodney* at Birmingham Railway Museum in 2009. The locomotive is in need of major mechanical repairs in addition to attention to its bodywork.

The bodyshell of 50026 *Indomitable* resting on stands at MOD Bicester in 2004 during its extensive eighteen-year restoration.

50026 *Indomitable* on display at Kidderminster Town on the Severn Valley Railway for a diesel gala in 2009. The locomotive was visiting the railway for mechanical testing and running-in.

50026 *Indomitable* bursts into life at Haworth on the Keighley & Worth Valley Railway during a diesel gala in 2012.

50026 *Indomitable* at Wansford on the Nene Valley Railway during a diesel gala in 2012.

50027 *Lion* about to leave Grosmont on the North Yorkshire Moors Railway in 2006.

50027 *Lion* light engine at Goathland on the North Yorkshire Moors Railway during a diesel gala in 2006.

50027 *Lion* leaving Goathland for Pickering on the North Yorkshire Moors Railway during a diesel gala in 2007.

50027 *Lion* stops at Ropley on the Mid Hants Railway in 2012 on its inaugural passenger run, having returned from its extended stay at the North Yorkshire Moors Railway.

50027 *Lion* waits for the signal at Medstead and Four Marks on the Mid Hants Railway in 2012.

50029 *Renown* stored at Peak Rail in Derbyshire.

50029 *Renown* awaits restoration at Peak Rail in Derbyshire in 2005.

50029 *Renown* in 2007 after its cosmetic restoration to make it look more presentable to visitors, a condition of its acceptance at Peak Rail.

50030 *Repulse* in 2005 after its cosmetic restoration at Peak Rail.

50030 *Repulse* undergoing its long-term restoration at Peak Rail.

50031 *Hood* at the end of the line at Rhymney in 2005. The locomotive took part in the Arriva Trains Wales celebrations to mark the end of locomotive-hauled service trains on the Cardiff–Rhymney Valley commuter route.

50031 *Hood* stands just outside Leyburn on the Wensleydale Railway during 'The Redmire Rambler' rail tour in 2006.

50031 *Hood* and 50049 *Defiance* at Kingussie during 'The Orcadian' rail tour in 2006. Both locomotives had temporarily been given alter egos on one side only, with 50031 displaying 50028 *Tiger* and 50049 displaying 50012 *Benbow*.

50031 *Hood* at Inverness in 2006.

50031 *Hood* at Fishguard Harbour. Both this locomotive and 50049 *Defiance* were leased to Arriva Trains Wales in order to provide motive power for regular service trains from Cardiff–Fishguard during the summer of 2006.

50031 *Hood* at Kidderminster Town on the Severn Valley Railway. Now no longer main line certified, 50031 resides at the Severn Valley Railway, where it and the rest of The Fifty Fund fleet are based.

50031 *Hood* light engine in the head-shunt at Bridgnorth on the Severn Valley Railway.

50033 *Glorious* on display at STEAM museum in 2006.

50033 *Glorious* at Birmingham Railway Museum, having recently arrived from its previous home at STEAM museum.

50035 *Ark Royal* (fictitiously renumbered 50135) on display at Eastleigh Works open day in 2009, after having undergone a lengthy series of major mechanical repairs. This livery was never actually carried by the Class, but gives an idea of what they may have looked like had the Railfreight experiment in 1987 with 50149 been more successful.

50035 *Ark Royal* in the head-shunt at Bridgnorth on the Severn Valley Railway during a diesel gala in 2009.

50035 *Ark Royal* runs light engine through Highley on the Severn Valley Railway.

50035 *Ark Royal* about to leave Wansford on the Nene Valley Railway during a diesel gala in 2010.

50035 *Ark Royal* runs round the coaching stock at Rawtenstall on the East Lancashire Railway during a diesel gala in 2011.

50040 *Leviathan* (later renamed *Centurion*) at Coventry Railway Centre in 2005. The locomotive resided here for a number of years. Its condition was little more than a rotting shell on scrap bogies, with many of its large components removed.

50040 *Leviathan* at Coventry Railway Centre in 2005.

50040 *Leviathan* at Coventry Railway Centre. During 2008 it was the subject of a final search for remaining spare parts, and was then sold for scrap. It is pictured here being winched onto a low-loader on its final journey – to the scrapyard.

50042 *Triumph* (as 50006 *Neptune*) rests at Bodmin General on the Bodmin & Wenford Railway in 2006.

50042 *Triumph* rests at Bodmin General on the Bodmin & Wenford Railway during a diesel gala in 2006. The locomotive had just been newly overhauled and repainted in a British Rail corporate blue livery.

50042 *Triumph* (as 50039 *Implacable*) at Bodmin General on the Bodmin & Wenford Railway in 2009. 50042 was requested as the locomotive of choice for a private diesel charter in May 2009. It masqueraded as a now scrapped member of the class, having the TOPS number and nameplate 50039 *Implacable* affixed to its bodyside.

50044 *Exeter* (as D444) at Bewdley on the Severn Valley Railway in 2005. Externally, 50044 has been cosmetically restored to close to an ex-delivery condition by the removal of the high-intensity headlight and the restoring of the sandbox covers, roof cut-in and glass headcode panels. Until fairly recently, the locomotive sported its original number of D444 and a non-authentic British Rail two-tone green livery.

English Electric leasing plate on the bodyside of 50044 *Exeter*.

50044 *Exeter* rolls into Arley on the Severn Valley Railway during a diesel gala in 2008.

50044 *Exeter* rests in the head-shunt at Rawtenstall on the East Lancashire Railway during a diesel gala in 2011. This was the first outing for 50044 since it had been repainted back into its original BR Corporate Blue livery.

50044 *Exeter* at Llandudno Junction in 2011. Having become re-certified for use on the main line, 50044 was used on 'The Snowdon Ranger' two-day rail tour, run by PTG Tours in 2011.

50044 *Exeter* at Paignton in 2012. The locomotive was used on a GB Railfreight (GBRf) staff private charter that ran from Cardiff to Paignton. A mini-rail tour then followed from Paignton to Plymouth and the return. This was open to the general public, with all proceeds going to Age UK, the nominated GBRf charity for 2012.

50044 *Exeter* at Newton Abbot in 2012.

50049 *Defiance* at Bristol Temple Meads during the 'West Somerset Wanderer' rail tour in 2005.

50049 *Defiance* stands gleaming in the sun at Bridgnorth on the Severn Valley Railway during a diesel gala in 2011. The locomotive had very recently undergone bodywork repairs, resulting in its complete repaint with a distinctive black roof.

50049 *Defiance* and 50044 *Exeter* prepare to leave Edinburgh on 'The Edinburgh Explorer II' rail tour in 2011. 50049 is currently one of only two preserved Class 50s that are main line certified.

50050 *Fearless* undergoing long-term restoration at Yeovil Railway Centre in 2006.

50050 *Fearless* at Yeovil Railway Centre in 2010.

ENGLISH ELECTRIC TYPE 5 CO-CO (BRITISH RAIL CLASS 55 OR 'DELTIC'): 1961–1982

The Class 55 (Deltic) locomotives, built by English Electric between 1961 and 1962 and eventually numbering just twenty-two, were perhaps the most iconic diesel locomotives ever to run on the national network.

55002 *The King's Own Yorkshire Light Infantry* on static display at the National Railway Museum.

The prototype Deltic, one of the earliest main-line diesel locomotives, had entered service with British Rail (BR) in October 1955. Although officially numbered DP1 (Diesel Prototype 1), this was never carried on the locomotive, it being emblazoned instead with the word DELTIC in large cream letters on its powder-blue sides. Plans to name the locomotive 'Enterprise' never came to fruition, and it was forever known to everyone as 'Deltic', named after its iconic power units.

The design of DP1 was radical, employing the use of two 1,650-hp Napier Deltic high-speed engines that were high-powered, light and relatively small in size. Originally these engines had been developed for marine applications in the late 1940s, but English Electric recognised the potential in the Napier engine. The Deltic engine was an opposed-piston two-stroke diesel engine designed and produced by Napier & Son. The cylinders were divided into three blocks in a triangular arrangement, the blocks forming sides with crankshafts located in each apex of the triangle in the form of the Greek letter delta.

The locomotive first saw service on the London Euston–Liverpool Lime Street route on the London Midland Region of British Railways. However, the need to electrify the major routes on that region soon became apparent. This being the case, in 1959 DP1 was moved to the Eastern Region, which wanted to test the locomotive on its East Coast Mainline (ECML) express services between London King's Cross and Doncaster, where its top speed of 105 mph could be used to good effect.

A severe phasing gear oil leak saw the locomotive declared a failure in November 1960, which ultimately resulted in it being withdrawn officially in March 1961, by which time the production Class 55 locomotives were coming into service. It was returned to the English Electric Vulcan Foundry having completed 450,000 successful miles in service. A project to repair the locomotive and move it to Canada, with hopes of a subsequent export order, came to nothing. Instead the locomotive was donated to the Science Museum in London as part of its transport exhibition.

A review of the museum's collection in the 1980s led to a new home being sought, and it was the National Railway Museum (NRM) in York that provided accommodation for the locomotive, which arrived there in October 1993.

55002 *The King's Own Yorkshire Light Infantry* at the National Railway Museum, Shildon, during the Deltic 50 celebrations in 2011.

An order for twenty-two production Deltics, to replace fifty-five Gresley Pacific steam locomotives, was placed in 1958. Originally this had been for twenty-three locomotives, but the BTC gave approval for the lower number. This small fleet of English Electric Type 5 Co-Co locomotives, initially numbered in the range D9000–D9021, were built at the English Electric Vulcan Foundry in Newton-le-Willows between 1961 and 1962. The production versions, while being 7 tons lighter, were over 3 feet longer, with a bodyside contour that was swept in below the waist to improve clearances. Gone was the huge headlight of the original Deltic, but the typical English Electric nose was retained with a single, centrally positioned four-character headcode box. All emerged painted in a predominantly Brunswick green livery, with a contrasting lime green lower band, creamy white cab surrounds and a large centrally positioned British Railways logo. With the exception of the final two deliveries, class members lacked a high visibility warning on their front ends – a square yellow warning panel was applied at a later date.

Delivery of the first locomotive was almost a year later than contracted, with D9001 being the first into traffic in late February 1961. It was followed a few days later in the same month by D9000, which had been held back by English Electric while it was fitted with an experimental flashing warning light. Within weeks, however, the first two examples, together with newly delivered D9002 and D9003, were officially stopped, as problems had been found with fractures on their bogie transoms and loose rubbing plates. Having cured this problem, the remainder of the fleet began to be delivered at a rate of approximately two per month, with D9021 finally arriving in Doncaster for acceptance testing in mid-March 1962.

Their introduction on the ECML transformed services between London and Edinburgh – not unsurprising, since at the time of their construction they were the most powerful single-unit diesel locomotives in the world. Their introduction led to a step change in locomotive performance on the line. The recently introduced English Electric Type

4 (Class 40) locomotives had a continuous rating at rail horsepower of only 1,550 hp, which could be exceeded by a Pacific steam locomotive if worked hard. In contrast, the Deltics produced an at rail continuous rating of 2,640 hp. As early as 1963, Deltics were recorded exceeding 100 mph, which for 1963 was very impressive. The fact that the class achieved high utilisation rates helped to keep the ECML as the premier route in terms of speed for two decades.

Despite the extensive testing of the prototype, teething problems remained with the bogies of production versions. A considerable incidence of fatigue cracking remained in the transoms of the bogies, which indicated a possible design weakness. A new cast-steel bogie design had begun to be fitted in late 1964 to the final sixty examples of the English Electric Type 3 Co-Co (Class 37) locomotive. This appeared to rectify the problems experienced with the fabricated bogies, and these were fitted to all Deltics, beginning with D9011 in mid-1965 and finishing with D9008 five months later.

The Napier engines also experienced several problems – some of which continued to plague the class almost to their end. Indeed, in the second decade of service between 1973 and 1979, there were 270 engine failures, of which 95 were attributed to cylinder liners and seals, 92 attributed to pistons and 40 to quill shafts. Problems with the cylinder liners seemed to be multifactorial. Although a different coolant began to be used on the suggestion of English Electric, BR refused to treat the water in the steam-heat boiler, even though the engine cooling system could be topped up from this supply. Piston failures tended to be due to manufacturing faults, and ultrasonic testing was used to counter the issue, given the potentially catastrophic consequences to the engine should a piston fail.

Unwelcome characteristics of the design were their very high noise levels, and the quantity of exhaust fumes emitted by their twin two-stroke engines. The noise level was certainly an issue for lineside dwellers, passengers at stations and the drivers themselves. The deep droning noise heard in the cab was such that, for a time, crew were issued with ear protectors to combat the noise, pending better sound insulation.

Several updates and improvements were made to the class during their working lives. In 1968, air-braked carriages began to be introduced to the ECML. This required the class to be dual braked, and so, between the period October 1967 and July 1968, class members were duly fitted with the necessary equipment. A few years prior to this upgrade, BR had decided to introduce Electric Train Heating (ETH) on its carriages. Plans as to how this would be achieved on the Deltics began as early as 1965; this was not a simple matter, due to the very cramped nature of the internal working environment and the lack of space to fit another

55002 *The King's Own Yorkshire Light Infantry* sits proudly on the turntable at Wansford on the Nene Valley Railway during a diesel gala in 2012.

generator. However, a design was approved whereby power could be sourced from the main generator itself, and suitable modifications were made to all members of the class during 1970–1.

With the introduction of the BR Total Operations Processing System (TOPS) in 1973, the locomotives were designated Class 55 and renumbered accordingly in sequence 55001–55022, with D9000 becoming 55022 due to a limitation of the system.

In 1975, investigations began, starting with 55016, regarding the viability of a light refurbishment of the fleet to prepare the class for a further five to ten years in front-line operation. A total rewiring was undertaken, but in the process it was found to be largely unnecessary. Attention was given to the bodywork outer skin and the cab door surrounds, the now redundant headcode was blanked off, and two domino lights were added. The cab side

55002 *The King's Own Yorkshire Light Infantry* about to leave Bridgnorth on the Severn Valley Railway. This was the first time for over a decade that a

windows were also modified to address complaints of leaks and draughts in this area, and to address this the leading triangular window was removed and replaced with metal. This general repair work began on four other class members to a greater or lesser extent, after which further overhauls were restricted to incorporating only the most necessary modifications required.

Withdrawals of class members began with 55001 *St Paddy* and 55020 *Nimbus* in January 1980, although both locomotives had been out of service since early 1978. The final months of service were met by almost mass hysteria from the enthusiast population. British Rail, having had experience of planning farewell tours for the Western diesel-hydraulics, therefore devised a programme of farewell tours to mark the end of an era. The last Deltic-hauled service on a BR service train was given to 55019 *Royal Highland Fusilier* on 31 December 1981, after which all remaining class members were immediately withdrawn, with the exception of those planned for use on the last farewell tour.

The final tour, 'The Deltic Scotsman Farewell' from London to Edinburgh and back, took place a couple of days later on 2 January 1982. Hauled by 55015 *Tulyar* on the outward leg and 55022 *Royal Scots Grey* on the return, the route was lined with huge numbers of enthusiasts, with the platforms at Doncaster, York, Newcastle and Darlington stations full to overflowing with those wishing to pay their last respects. The chaotic scenes when 55022 returned to London King's Cross that evening were filmed by an ITN film crew and made the national news that night. They captured the moment when one emotional enthusiast sank down on his knees and kissed the locomotive goodbye.

All of the Class 55 fleet (Deltic) met their demise at Doncaster Works – the place where they had previously gone to be repaired. The very last example to be cut up was 55004 *Queen's Own Highlander* in July 1983. Currently, six examples from the original total of twenty-two survive, most in an operational condition, with two examples certified for use on the national mainline.

55002 *The King's Own Yorkshire Light Infantry* about to leave on the first service of the day from Kidderminster Town on the Severn Valley Railway, during a diesel gala in 2013.

55009 *Alycidon* (as D9009) on static display at the National Railway Museum (NRM) during a Sixties-themed event in 2008.

55009 *Alycidon* poses at Wansford on the Nene Valley Railway during a diesel gala in 2009. Even though I am too young to remember them in this livery, I must admit to having a preference for this over the British Rail corporate blue.

55009 *Alycidon* starts up one of its Napier Deltic engines at Loughborough Central on the Great Central Railway in 2010.

55009 *Alycidon* runs around the coaching stock at Bewdley on the Severn Valley Railway during a diesel gala in 2013.

55009 *Alycidon* in the head-shunt at Bridgnorth on the Severn Valley Railway. Notice the addition of a high-intensity headlight to the cab front now that this locomotive is main line certified once again.

55015 *Tulyar* (as D9015) nears the final stages of its extensive overhaul at Barrow Hill Roundhouse near Chesterfield in 2010. The locomotive appears to be in an as-new condition.

55015 *Tulyar* at the National Railway Museum, Shildon, during the Deltic 50 celebrations in 2011.

55016 *Gordon Highlander* (as D9016) at Birmingham Railway Museum in 2005. Here the locomotive still retains its disfiguring WIPAC light clusters from when it had been operated on the mainline by Deltic 9000 Locomotives Limited (DNLL) and Porterbrook Leasing.

55016 *Gordon Highlander* at a very cold Rawtenstall on the East Lancashire Railway in 2010. This was one of its first runs after changing ownership and being relocated to this railway. The WIPAC light clusters have been removed, and its original tail lamps reinstated.

55016 *Gordon Highlander* and 55022 *Royal Scots Grey* make an impressive line-up at the East Lancashire Railway during the Deltics 50 Years Gala special event in 2011.

55016 *Gordon Highlander* at the National Railway Museum, Shildon, during the Deltic 50 celebrations in 2011.

55016 *Gordon Highlander* at Bury Bolton Street on the East Lancashire Railway during an English Electric-themed day in 2014.

55019 *Royal Highland Fusilier* in profile at Leicester North on the Great Central Railway in 2009.

55019 *Royal Highland Fusilier* about to depart Quorn & Woodhouse on the Great Central Railway during a diesel gala in 2009.

55019 *Royal Highland Fusilier* light engine in the yard at Wansford on the Nene Valley Railway in 2012.

55019 *Royal Highland Fusilier* ready to depart Wansford on the Nene Valley Railway during a diesel gala in 212.

55019 *Royal Highland Fusilier* and 55009 *Alycidon* (as D9009) at Didcot Railway Centre during a diesel gala in 2013.

55022 *Royal Scots Grey* at Rugby in 2011. 55022 is currently one of three preserved Class 55 Deltics that are main line certified, the others being 55002 *The King's Own Yorkshire Light Infantry* and 55009 *Alycidon*.

55022 *Royal Scots Grey* at the buffer-stops at London Euston in 2011 as part of a positioning move for a rail tour.

55022 *Royal Scots Grey* arrives in Edinburgh during 'The Royal Scots Grey' rail tour in 2011.

55022 *Royal Scots Grey* and 55016 *Gordon Highlander* (as D9016) double-heading through Ramsbottom on the East Lancashire Railway during the Deltics 50 Years Gala special event in 2011.

THE ENGLISH ELECTRIC COMPANY L^{TD}.
LONDON
N° 2905/D557. 1960.
THE VULCAN FOUNDRY L^{TD}
LOCOMOTIVE WORKS, ENGLAND.

English Electric builder's plate on the bodyside of 55022 *Royal Scots Grey*.

55022 *Royal Scots Grey* at Rawtenstall on the East Lancashire Railway during an English Electric-themed day in 2012.

An impressive line-up at the Deltic 50 event in 2011. To mark the fiftieth anniversary of the British Rail Class 55 Deltics' introduction on to the East Coast Main Line (ECML), The National Railway Museum at Shildon and The Deltic Preservation Society (DPS) celebrated with a special event. For the first time ever, all six surviving production Deltics, along with the prototype locomotive DELTIC, were brought together in one place.

DELTIC at the National Railway Museum, Shildon, during the Deltic 50 celebrations in 2011.

DELTIC bodyside English Electric roundel.

DELTIC cab detail showing the US-style front headlight.

DELTIC painted nameplate.

Plaque on the bodyside of DELTIC.

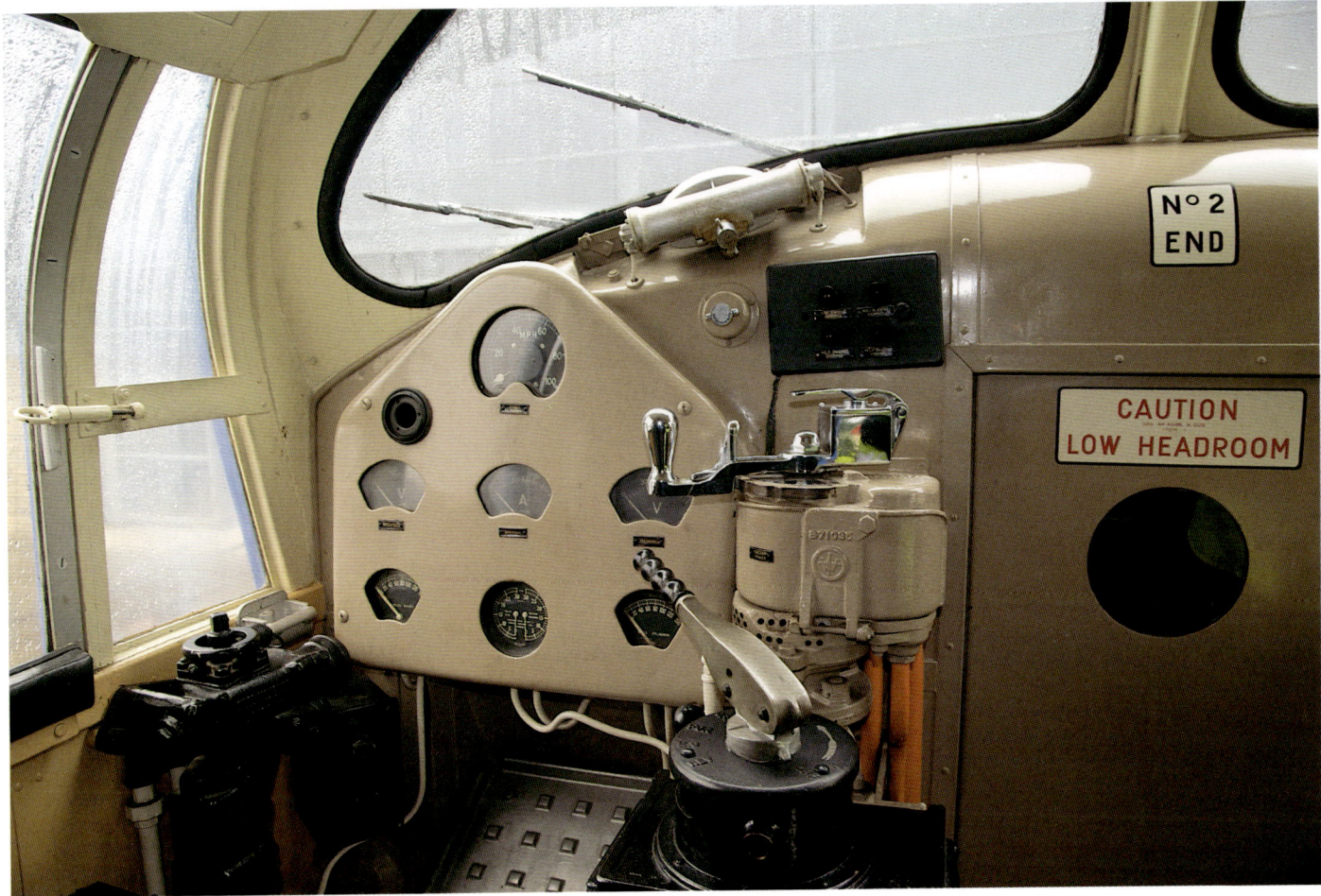

Cab detail of DELTIC showing the almost art deco styling.

THE FIFTY FUND

The Fifty Fund was founded in 1989 in an attempt to preserve an English Electric Type 4 (British Railways Class 50) locomotive in working order, since it seemed unlikely at the time that many of these complex locomotives would be saved.

In less than three years, sufficient capital was raised to purchase 50035 *Ark Royal* and 50044 *Exeter*, together with an extensive supply of spare parts. In addition, 50031 *Hood* was purchased by a small number of shareholders for operation by The Fifty Fund.

In 2006, The Fifty Fund merged its ownership and maintenance operations with Project Defiance, the owners of locomotive 50049 *Defiance*. This new combined organisation became known as The Class 50 Alliance. At the same time, The Fifty Fund became a fundraising organisation, a repository for the history of the class and a focal point for discussion of all aspects of its history.

The Fifty Fund continues to operate a share purchase by instalments scheme, with all shareholders in the Class 50 Alliance automatically becoming members of The Fifty Fund. Its fleet of locomotives are based at the Severn Valley Railway, which is widely regarded as one of the premier preserved railways in the UK. The railway also runs a series of driver experience courses on selected dates throughout the year, allowing you the opportunity to actually drive one of these locomotives. For more details contact Severn Valley Railway at www.svr.co.uk.

Should you wish to find out more about membership, buying shares or becoming more involved in volunteering work, please contact us:

The Fifty Fund
20 the Sycamores
Bluntisham
Cambridgeshire
PE28 3XW

Website: www.fiftyfund.org.uk

Sales: www.sales.fiftyfund.org.uk

The author at the controls of 50035 *Ark Royal* during a driver experience course at the Severn Valley Railway in 2012.